Discover the "Secret Formula" that the Most Successful CPA's & Accountants Use to Fuel Growth and Outperform the Competition

CA-TA-SA© System: The 1-Page Copyrighted Marketing Strategy for CPA's & Accountants. Powered by R4 Framework.

How to Integrate These 7 Systems & Technologies to Dominate Your Market & Ensure 25 Percent Growth or More in Your Firm in the Next 12 Months!

By: Mike Saunders, MBA

© 2015 Marketing Huddle, LLC
All Rights Reserved
ISBN 10:   1505667062
ISBN 13:   978-1505667066

All Rights Reserved. No part of this publication may be reproduced in any form or by any means, including scanning, photocopying, or otherwise without prior written permission of the copyright holder.

Disclaimer and Terms of Use: The Author and Publisher has strived to be as accurate and complete as possible in the creation of this book, notwithstanding the fact that he does not warrant or represent at any time that the contents within are accurate due to the rapidly changing nature of the Internet. While all attempts have been made to verify information provided in this publication, the Author and Publisher assumes no responsibility for errors, omissions, or contrary interpretation of the subject matter herein. Any perceived slights of specific persons, peoples, or organizations are unintentional. In practical advice books, like anything else in life, there are no guarantees of income made. Readers are cautioned to rely on their own judgment about their individual circumstances to act accordingly. This book is not intended for use as a source of legal, business, accounting or financial advice. All readers are advised to seek services of competent professionals in legal, business, accounting, and finance field.

Mike Saunders holds an MBA in Marketing and serves the small and medium-sized business market. In addition to coaching and consulting clients in his firm Marketing Huddle, he teaches Marketing Strategy as an Adjunct Marketing Professor at several Universities.

"I am a Brand Optimization Expert & I help CPA's & Accountants who specialize in Tax Resolution, with my copyrighted system: called "CA-TA-SA©" to make sure that your business growth is maximized by: Reputation, Reach, Resell and Referral. Optimizing any of the 4R's can produce 25% of annual business growth, but maximizing all 4 provides a compounding effect with Strategy, Tactics & Execution.

Mike Saunders, MBA
Business Strategist | Marketing Fanatic
Mike@MarketingHuddle.com
www.MarketingHuddle.com
www.Linkedin.com/in/MikeSaundersMBA

Table of Contents

Welcome!	1
Designing a Strategic Marketing Blueprint	3
Competitive Advantage	5
Target Audience	23
Strategic Alliances	43
Dramatic Changes in the Marketplace	51
Renewed Focus on the Fundamentals!	65
What are you missing?	77
Is your business being left behind?	79
What Are You Doing to Optimize the Four R's?	85

Welcome!

What I'm about to show you can ignite growth at your business well beyond the levels you've likely achieved in the past. If you specialize in Tax Resolution, this strategy will work because you must differentiate yourself from the competition. How do I know this is true?

Because a HUGE percent of the clients I have worked with over the years are missing AT LEAST two out of the four critical, proven marketing systems that are necessary to achieve maximum business growth.

So unless your situation is completely out of the ordinary (which is possible but unlikely), **there is a really big opportunity to accelerate the growth of your business**.

And the acceleration I'm talking about isn't a short-lived "sugar-rush" kind of growth. It's the sustainable and responsible kind—the kind that complements your ethical standards and supports your long-term vision for your business.

Skeptical?

I understand. But as you continue reading, you'll discover that the 7 systems & technologies I'm talking about aren't gimmicky, revolutionary or impossible to implement.

They don't require you to turn your business model upside down or become something you're not.

They are simply:
1. **C**ompetitive **A**dvantage
2. **T**arget **A**udience
3. **S**trategic **A**lliances
4. **R**eputation
5. **R**each
6. **R**esell
7. **R**eferral

In fact, *these elements are the foundational building blocks that every successful business must optimize in order to achieve the growth they're looking for*. But again, my experience tells me that most businesses are not taking complete (or efficient) advantage of each of the pieces.

I help CPA's & Accountants who specialize in Tax Resolution reach their growth potential and dominate their markets by implementing proven marketing systems. Think about it, if someone is having issues with the IRS and they go to Google (who doesn't!) how crowded is THAT space?! And how credible are your competitors? You can stand head and shoulders above the rest with a Reputation Management and Marketing Strategy.

My job is to be an expert in marketing, and specifically local marketing that leverages technology to achieve maximum results, so that my clients can focus on what they do best!

I've got a lot to share with you about how CPA's & Accountants can dominate their market and take their income to entirely new levels.

Designing a Strategic Marketing Blueprint for Your Accounting Firm

After years of consulting with business owners on their Marketing Strategy a pattern began to appear. I found that we were focusing on specific points in building out their strategy and each one built upon the previous. As I began to research these strategies, a simple system appeared that delivered powerful results. Once I began to walk the client through the steps, I drew 3 boxes on a Legal pad and it opened up vast amounts of opportunities for us to grow their business. The simplicity of the "boxes" is what gives it the powerful results, because anything that becomes cumbersome…doesn't get done! I call my copyrighted system "CA-TA-SA©" relating to the 3-box coaching system I created which is a fusion of Competitive Advantage, Target Audience and Strategic Alliances. This strategy is enhanced by the R4 Framework. Optimizing any of the 4R's of Reputation, Reach, Resell and Referral can produce 25% of annual business growth, but maximizing all 4 provides a compounding effect with Strategy, Tactics & Execution & you get an MBA-level marketing strategy for your business. Then ALL of your marketing will resonate powerfully with your target audience so that they fully understand why you are the obvious choice!

Let's get started!

Competitive Advantage

What is a Unique Selling Proposition and Why Do You Need One?

Your Competitive Advantage is summed up in a precise unique selling proposition (USP) which is a statement that explains how your business is different from everyone else in the market. It tells your customers how you can better meet their needs and what makes you special. Your USP essentially tells them why they should buy from you instead of from your competitors. It takes some creativity to come up with a compelling USP, but it's the biggest decision you'll ever make for your business. In essence, it defines why you are the Obvious Choice!

Why You Need A USP

The simple reason that you need a USP is that, no matter what product you're selling to which market, there are other companies you're competing with, and you need to stand out. You want your market to think of YOU when they need your products or services. If you create a good USP, it will stick in their memory and put you above the rest.

The Elements of a Good USP

There are three things that make a good USP:

1. It specifically addresses the needs of your market. It should be something they can't live without, that solves their problems, or makes their lives easier.

2. A good USP is memorable. It has to stick in people's minds so that you're the one they think of when they need your products.

3. It connects with your buyers emotionally. Good USP's speak to the fears, worries, desires, and frustrations of your target market. Remember that people make decisions logically but buy based on emotion!

A huge aspect of knowing your target market is conducting good market research. In my classes I teach, we talk about primary and secondary research. The main differences are: primary research is conducted by you and secondary is research that is already done on markets similar to your target audience. Primary research can be more expensive and time-consuming, although, if you have cultivated a great email list of your clients you can easily create a survey and send it out very affordably!

A good USP is especially essential in a crowded market. If you're up against a large number of competitors, you need an especially strong USP to cut through the noise. On the other hand, even if your business is the only game in town, you still need to create a USP that speaks to your audience. It's not only about battling the competition, but also establishing your brand in the minds of your customers. This is one of the 4 P's of marketing (Positioning), and is essential to understand because you can "own market share" in the minds of your target audience! I have heard it said that good marketing is like "buying brain cells" in the sense that even if your email is deleted, for example, the moment the recipient took to see it was from you and the subject line, they actually thought of you! This is even more powerful when they open it to give the email a quick read.

Failing to Plan is Planning to Fail

Amazingly, a majority of those who start their own businesses fail to create a unique selling proposition. Of those who don't, many fail. However, creating a USP that suits your business and speaks to your audience doesn't automatically guarantee success. Your products or services need to deliver on the promise that your USP is making. Otherwise, it won't get you very far.

The Creative Process

Your unique selling proposition won't appear out of thin air. Since this is such an important decision, it's a process that takes some time. However, it's not difficult to come up with the right message if you follow certain steps. Pay attention to your market, check out your competitors, and analyze your products to find their unique selling point. If you put in the time and refine as necessary, you can create the right USP for your business. Many business owners find that they are just too close to the business to think objectively. The success that can be achieved by working with a Business Coach is powerful.

Step 1: Understand Your Target Market

In order to create a winning USP, you need to understand the people in your target market at an individual level. This means not as a mass of demographic statistics, but as actual human beings. Your USP needs to appeal to their needs and desires, as well as their frustrations, worries, problems, and pain points. When you connect in this way, you create an emotional bond. The first step is getting to know these individuals. What "keeps them up at night"? What is something that would solve a specific problem to make their life dramatically easier? When you can identify the gap between where they want to be in their life or business and where they are now, you can position your service as a way to close the gap and solve their problem.

Study Demographics

Start by looking at demographics. Find out your target customers' age, gender, occupation, education level, and income. Try to be as specific as possible. Although you may have a good idea about your target market's demographics, don't leave it up to guesswork. When creating a demographic profile, rely on hard data wherever possible. You can go to your local library to get access to very powerful computer programs that can shine light on your target audience and demographics.

But wait! You may be thinking that this is the section on Competitive Advantage and what makes your business stand out from the competition. Why are we jumping into demographics? It's like Steven Covey said in his book 7 Habits of Highly Effective People: "Begin with the end in mind"! You must understand your target audience so that you can effectively communicate your competitive advantage.

Observe Your Market

Gather data about your market online and offline. Online, you can use social media sites, forums, reviews and blogs. Find out where your customers hang out online and spend time there. Locate them on LinkedIn to see what groups they are in, and then join too! Offline data gathering methods include surveys and focus groups.

In addition to looking for demographic information, also look for psychological data. How do people in your market feel about themselves and the products they buy? Try to understand what makes them tick. This goes a long way to giving you insights on how to communicate to them in describing your services.

Engage Your Market in Conversation

Get into conversations with your target market to learn more about them. A common offline market research method is to conduct surveys. Surveys work well but they're one-sided. A better approach is to get a dialogue going. You can do this through social media sites like Facebook, online forums, or your blog. Engage people in conversation related to your product or just come right out and ask them how they feel about it. Think of it this way, don't you feel a bit more free and empowered to speak your mind when you are doing it from behind your computer screen? If you were approached in person at the mall or at your front door, it would be a completely different story! Take this thought and implement it in your research process, you will find that it will make it easy to get opinions.

Take Good Notes

When conducting market research, it's important to take good notes. Record all of the data you gather and organize it so that it's easy to analyze. Separate data into categories, such as demographics and psychology. Look for data that's consistent from one person to another. Try to find ways to quantify your results. When it comes to market research, objective data is the most important. Subjective data, such as someone's feelings about your product, should be used to support the objective data.

CA-TA-SA© System

Draw a Picture

Take all of the consistent trends you find and create a picture of your ideal customer. Identify their demographic information, their opinions, their buying habits, and all the other data you've gathered. Once you've done this, it's much easier to create a unique selling proposition. You now have a good idea of what your customers want and need in the products they buy. You can write your USP so that it speaks directly to those wants and needs.

You can even look at the physical picture you've drawn as you're doing your writing, so that it sounds as realistic and personal as possible. You can even name your "persona" so that while you are working on marketing campaigns you can make sure you are connecting directly with "Emma" (or whatever name you choose!) I heard an example of a company that did this and printed off the picture and description of their ideal customer avatar/persona and placed it on top of each computer of each employee in the office. This was a powerful way to keep everyone focused on who they are serving!

An Edge on the Competition

Armed with all of this information about your target market, you'll have an edge over the competition. It'll be easy to see what mistakes they are making and how they are not delivering. You and your company can then fill in the gaps and give your market exactly what they want.

Step 2: Spying on Your Competitors

One of the key elements of a good USP is that it's unique. It offers something nobody else in the marketplace is offering. In order to come up with something unique, you need to know exactly what your competitors are offering so that you can offer something that's more attractive or valuable for your target market. Study your competitors' products and strategies so that you can create something that really stands out.

Research Products

Spend time researching your competitors' products. If possible, buy them and use them yourself. In particular, look at how they meet (or don't meet) the needs of your customers. Stay up-to-date on each new product line your competitor introduces. It also helps to understand how your market feels about your competitors' products, so keep your eyes and ears out for any mentions of them.

Study Their Marketing

Gather your competitors' marketing materials and study them. Look at which benefits they are emphasizing to their customers. Make sure you pay attention to the specific language and communication methods your competitors use to relate to their customers. Is it more casual or more formal? Do they focus more on visuals or audio materials?

Take a look at the channels your competitors use for marketing also, since that's where your customers are.

What different marketing methods are your competitors using in each channel? You're going to try to do something different with your message, so you need to have a very clear understanding of what your competitors are already saying. The last thing you want to be is a copycat.

And don't forget to look at the keywords your competitors are targeting since that will show you exactly which search terms you might have to compete for, or which ones you want to avoid.

Understand the Relationship with Their Customers

Find out what your competitors' customers think about them. Look at websites that have customer reviews of their products. Search for the company's name on related forums. You can often turn up information by simply searching your competitor's name in Google along with related terms like 'great deal' or 'terrible.' Especially when customers are dissatisfied, you can discover areas where you can excel. Another easy tip is to set up a Google Alert so that anytime your competitors are mentioned online, you will get an email! You can do this for a handful of competitors to keep updated on their activity.

Customer Service Considerations

Even if you offer similar products in a similar way, customer service is one area in which it's easy to excel over the competition. When researching your competitors, pay attention to how they treat their customers and how their customers feel about it. If you have better customer service, this is an incredible edge.

Your Competitors' Report Card

After you've gathered all of your information and checked out your competitors everywhere possible, add up all the data. Create a 'report card' for your competitor that shows where they excel and where they fall short. Take a look at your strengths and weaknesses and compare.

Your company's natural strengths – the areas where you excel without necessarily trying – offer the best starting point for creating your USP. For example, if you're naturally faster at what you do than the competition, this is a good point to emphasize.

Online Tools

This type of competitive research used to be time consuming and expensive, but now it's incredibly fast and easy, because most of it can be done through the Internet. Find your competition everywhere you can online and follow everything they do. You don't need to pay money to conduct surveys or focus groups. With social media and online forums, you can simply find your competitors and be a fly on the wall. You can sit back and observe, and the market will tell you everything you need to know.

Step 3: Create a Product That Blows Away the Competition

A unique selling proposition is only going to get you so far if you don't have a great product behind it. Your product needs to live up to the promise of your USP, surpassing other products on the market and providing the customer with unique benefits.

Review Your Research

By this time, you've researched your market and your competitors, and you should have a stack of data. It's time to analyze this data to discover exactly what your customers want and how your competition is meeting their needs.

Make a chart and do a side-by-side comparison of your products with those of the competition. You should also examine your sales data and customer feedback.

When looking at this data, there are a few important questions to ask yourself:

- Do your current products and services uniquely address your customers' needs?

- What exactly is unique about your products and sets them apart from other products available to your customers?

- Where do your products and services fall short? Wherever there's a weakness, this is an area you can focus your energies on improving.

- How can you offer a solution to your customers that your competition isn't offering?

New and Improved

At this point, you'll need to ask yourself whether you can make improvements in your product or whether you need to develop something entirely new. Your analysis of your products' weaknesses along with customer feedback and sales figures will help you decide this. Sometimes, your current products can simply be repackaged and sold with the new USP.

If you need to develop something new, you can use your old product's weak points as the basis of the new product's USP. For example, maybe you have a software program that a number of your customers complain is complex and counter-intuitive. After you rebuild the program so that it's more user friendly, create a USP that says something along the lines of, 'You don't have to pull out your hair figuring it out how to use this!'

Laser-Target Your Market

One good way to differentiate your business is to choose a more specific sub-set of the market. Take a certain demographic of your market and laser-target it.

For example, if your products appeal to an age group that stretches from "twenty-something's" to over fifty, focus on one small part of that spectrum, such as customers in their early twenties. You can focus on a demographic subset based on anything – geographical location, language, economic status, occupation, family structure, etc.

Get Ideas from Established Brands

Another simple bit of research that can help you generate ideas is to look at other brands and their products and figure out what makes them unique. Pay attention to how they tailor their message to their target market.

Step 4: Create Your Unique Selling Proposition

You now have all the knowledge you need. It's time to put it all together and create a unique selling proposition that tells your laser-targeted market why they should buy from you.

In order to do this, here are a few questions to get your creative process started:

- Whose needs am I addressing? (Look at your target market's demographic information)

- What do I offer that no one else can?

- Why should people buy from me and not another company? (Note: this doesn't have to be based on your products. It could be your unique understanding of your customers, your delivery method, or extra services you offer)

Writing Your USP

The process of creating a USP involves brainstorming and refining. When brainstorming, get down as many ideas as possible and don't worry about which ones are good and which ones aren't. The goal is to come up with quantity. Later you'll narrow it down, and the more you have to consider, the better.

Tips for Writing Your USP

Keep It Short but Compelling. Your USP should be something your customers will 'get' immediately. After you've narrowed down your list, take each idea and see if you can trim it without losing the meaning or impact.

Test It. Test your USP on real people in your market and get feedback from them. Offer a small incentive like a freebie or discount for participating. Use their feedback to make tweaks. This is also a great way to deepen your relationship with them and to give people a sense of belonging to your beta group. Many times they become so connected to your brand because they were not only given an opportunity, but also you listened to their opinions and implemented some!

Why Be the Best?

One of the best USP strategies is to forget about telling your customers that you're the best. They'll find that out on their own. Create a USP that says, 'We may not be the best, but we're the only ones who…'_____
This tells your target market the unique benefit they'll get using your company as well as how you are different from the competition in a specific way. When you can point out a specific aspect of your service offering that speaks right to your target audience, because of your research, you win.

Target Audience

Knowing your customer's demographics is very, very important to your company, to your branding, and to your conversions. Let's say for example that your target audience demographics, or a majority of clients, are female, college level education, business owners and about 35 years old. But without knowing, you start trying to appeal to everybody, and what happens is this; let's say that you begin to create videos, create websites, and your marketing starts to appeal more to men, oops! That's an ideal situation that a lot of people face. See the problem here? So without the information, you really can't put a face to who your audience is, who your buyers are, and their gender, their age, the education level, the earning, the jobs that they might have where they could be located, their likes, their dislikes, and so forth.

So once you know the demographics, you can focus on the right audience that will increase your branding and conversions now as well as down the road. So you're really setting yourself up for success instead of jumping right in without doing the proper research and planning, and setting yourself up for failure. So we want to make sure that you set yourself up for success. This is not to say that you will not accept any clients that don't fit into this segment you are focusing on, quite the contrary! What you will find is that while you are focusing your messaging and marketing toward this segment of your target audience, it begins to resonate well with them and they engage with your brand. This allows you to be on the forefront of their mind as they interact with their sphere of influence and you have a dramatically better chance of receiving referrals!

Well, let me talk about the steps to figuring this out, and then I'm going to show you exactly how to go about doing this. First of all of course, you're going to need to know your niche market, your target market, or your topic. There are many tools you can use to get these data, such as Quantcast. A quick Google search will show you where to find this tool and you'll fins short videos on how to best use it. Quantcast is going to tell us the demographics of the visitors to a website. We're going to use this information to create a demographic profile to support our efforts in creating a target audience.

Simple research like this gives you an idea of who your target audience is, you can do more research on that demographic to see possible likes, possible dislikes, some sort of commonalities and things like that. Then and only then, should you begin to begin to start branding, and figuring out how can you appeal to this specific group.

So make sure you use this information, take some action and get the demographics of your ideal buyers! This is a perfect example of what I mentioned earlier about secondary research. These demographics and stats are not your specific clients but they should be similar enough that it gives you great insight into positioning your services to them!

Why Demographic and Geographic Data Isn't Enough

You put tremendous effort into your marketing strategy and plan. Each piece of content is finely crafted to get the best results. Your target audience is defined in your business plan and your marketing strategy. That research, information, and description is what you use to base your tactics on.

Unfortunately, if you're only using demographic and geographic information, you're missing out on potential connections and profits and you may even be marketing to the wrong people. That's a lot of wasted time, money, and effort.

Think about this…

The year that someone was born and where they live will not tell you if they are likely to buy your products or services. It's just not enough information. It's a start and it's a good start. But it isn't enough.

Let's use the example of a business coach. They might attract solo entrepreneurs and small business owners. Each group has their own unique needs and goals.

Content and marketing tactics need to be created for each audience. Let's imagine that you know the demographics and geographic information about your audience.

You know that your audience is women ages 25-40 who live in the Midwest and central United States and that most of them have at least a two year college degree.

Great. So you start creating content for women who are business owners in this age bracket and geographic region. But what if they're mostly conservative single moms? How does that change the picture? And what if these single mom business owners are high achievers? They're not struggling, they're goal oriented, and attracted to stable and compassionate brands.

This information changes the way you market to them, right? It gives you more information to brand, to build relationships, to market and to change how you offer your products or services.

As you can see, geographic data and demographic data are really just the tip of the iceberg. They're part of the bigger picture but only a small part. If you're not including psychographic information in your market research and in the creation of your definition of your target audience, you're missing out on the bulk of your most important intelligence.

It's also critical to understand that consumers have changed. The opportunity of choice and the vast amount of information available to consumers has modified the way they shop and do business. Today, consumers create their own solutions. A look at how they buy coffee is a perfect example.

Twenty or even ten years ago, if a person wanted a cup of coffee they ordered a cup of coffee. The server might ask if they wanted cream and sugar. Today, if you order a cup of coffee you have hundreds of possible combinations. The coffee consumer is able to create and order a coffee drink that fits their needs, mood, and budget. And as they order their coffee they're able to have a lovely conversation, if they choose, with the person that's taking their order.

This coffee example can be applied to just about any product or service purchase. Consumers are now researching their purchases and looking for solutions, often customizable solutions that fit their unique needs. Those needs may change from moment to moment as the world changes much more quickly now than ever before.

How people shop online and off has changed and that means that the more information you have about your audience, the better your marketing efforts. The big question now is how do you go about gathering this information about your audience? The process is called "Psychographic Profiling."

The Key Elements of Psychographic Profiling

The first step to gaining a better understanding of your market and target audience is to begin to create a profile of your customer. You likely already know many of the demographics and geographic information about your audience.

It's time to start compiling the psychographics. That means collecting three different key elements of data. Let's take a quick look at these and then we'll talk about the individual pieces.

Social Profile Data

Social profile data comes from social networks. It's comprised of all the fields social media users grant permission for brands to use on their behalf. For example, when you or your customer join a social network, you fill out fields or profile information like your relationship status, alma mater, interests, professional affiliations, and occupation. It often helps you define your audience's social class.

This information can be used to establish and build a closer relationship with your customers and prospects. Obtaining and gathering the information is the first step. There are tools and services that make this step easier.

For example, a tool called Full Contact lets you query by Twitter username, Facebook ID or other contact information to find and gather social media profile information. Keep in mind that social profile data is only useable if it's actionable and combined with other data.

Behavior Data

Behavior data allows you to measure and track how your audience behaves over time. It segments your market into groups based on their knowledge of your products and services, attitudes toward your brand, how they use your products or services and how they respond to your business.

Behavioral data is a lot of different data collected about an individual behavior for marketing purposes. Generally speaking, some common types of behavior data include:

- Data collected on behavioral ad networks - how people respond to ads
- Data collected on your website
- Comments and activity on social media sites

Behavioral data includes readiness, usage, and loyalty. It can be used to help personalize your content and marketing efforts. The goal when using behavior data is to help identify and clarify your market's interest and to know where they are in the sales funnel. The information can be used to segment and personalize offers, blog and website content and email messages.

Lifestyle Data

Lifestyle data is the process of gathering information about people's values, beliefs, interests, and opinions. There are different models that people follow and not one industry standard. The bottom line and most important factor to remember is that the information you're gathering and how you organize it must integrate with your other data and ultimately be information that you can take action on.

Market segmentation services are usually the 'go to' resource here for data collection. For example, Mosaic by Experian Marketing Services, provides segmentation insights into your audience's behavior, attitudes, and preferences. Surveys, polls, and other data-gathering devices can also help you collect this information.

Within each of these three key elements are individual pieces that need to be examined and defined for your target audience. For example, within lifestyle there are values, opinions, and beliefs. Let's take a look at these components by providing a working definition of what each is and why they're important.

The 10 Components of Psychographics
You now know that psychographics are essential to defining and understanding your target market. What you may not know is why each piece of information is important. In this section, we'll take a quick look at how psychographics reflect your target audience's living patterns and purchasing behavior and why each piece of information is important.

Psychographics gathers info on your audience's:

1. **Interests** – What is your audience interested in? Are they interested in pets, politics, entertainment or technology news? Your prospects' interests help you position and create the right marketing message. For example, if you have a prospect who's interested in politics, writing a headline that integrates entertainment news or gossip isn't going to work as well for them as an analogy to a political event.
2. **Opinions** – Opinions matter and your audience's opinions can spread quickly. It's important to both understand and manage your audience's opinions about your products or services so you can provide immediate feedback and an appropriate marketing response.
3. **Beliefs** – What do they believe? We're not just talking about religious beliefs. What do they believe about success, money, happiness and other elements of life? You can connect with shared beliefs or challenge their beliefs to get them to

open their mind to new ideas, products, and services.

4. **Values** – Your audience's values are their broad preferences concerning appropriate courses of action or outcomes. It's their sense of right and wrong and what's important to them. For example, do they value family over success? Do they value fame or fortune? Connect with your prospect's values to really engage with them.

5. **Goals** – What do they want to achieve? For example, are they a bargain hunter looking for the best price or are they oriented toward brand recognition? Understanding your prospects' goals can help you craft a message that speaks to them.

6. **Attitudes** - Attitudes play an important role in marketing content creation. An attitude is a positive or negative evaluation of people, events, act or ideas.

7. **Purchasing motives** – Why does your prospect make purchases? What is their motive? For example, are they motivated by fear of loss or by pride and prestige? Do they want to save money? Avoid pain? Feel comforted and connected?

8. **Personal characteristics** – Personality is difficult to measure but it can play a role in creating your customer's psychographic profile. For example, is your audience complacent or determined? Are they inquisitive? Are they demanding? This information can help you provide the content and information your audience needs to make a buying decision.

9. **Activities** – What does your prospect do? What are their hobbies? What are their travelling habits, working habits, and so on. How do they spend their weekdays and evenings? This information can help you craft personal messages and it can also help with the timing of your marketing messages.

10. **Social class** – Where does your customer or prospect fall on the socioeconomic scale? Are they a professional or a manual worker? The language you use and the products or services you provide can be promoted differently depending on the social class you're appealing to.

How to Use Psychographic Data in Your Marketing

Let's say that you've spent the time, energy, and money to gather all of the psychographic information about your audience. You now have an accurate understanding of who they are, how they behave, and why they behave the way they do. You know their needs, wants, and motivations. Now what? What do you do with all of that information?

You use the psychographic information you gather everywhere in your business! Every component of your marketing strategy is impacted by your customer profile. For example, your branding and unique value proposition can now speak directly to your customer's actual wants and needs.

How you package and promote your products and services can reflect the information and benefits that are most important to your audience. Your sales copy, blog content, email content right down to the headline and the language you use in your content all reflects the language and benefits that your prospects prioritize and understand.

Your call to action can even be fine-tuned to speak in a language that your prospect understands. Every aspect of your marketing strategy and plan are impacted by your psychographic information and a stronger understanding of who your audience really is.

Ways to Use Your Psychographic Data

Let's take a look at five different ways you can use your psychographic data in various areas of your marketing.

CA-TA-SA© System

1. Customer Profiles

When you begin crafting any marketing piece you need to always keep your customer in mind. You may have originally created a customer profile in your business plan. You may have only used demographic information to help define your profile, and maybe some guesses about psychographics.

With the additional research you've done, you now have more information to work with and can use your psychographic data to create one or more narrowly focused customer profiles. For example, you might have a work-at-home mom profile and a single dad profile. Both are customers but each has their unique characteristics.

Take a look through the data you gathered and look for ways to divide up your customers into distinct profiles, or personas. Any time you start saying that you appeal to 'this group' AND 'that group', you probably need two different customer profiles.

The important thing is to look for key differences, commonalities, and trends in the needs, personalities, behaviors and other psychographic data. During the process, you'll also be able to start ruling out characteristics that are NOT part of your target market's profile too. Those elements are just as important to keep in mind. For example, your market may respond better to casual language and be turned off by formal or pretentious-sounding words.

2. List Segmentation

Using your new and improved customer profiles you can now apply that information to your customer database and email lists. For example, an email to single dads might be quite different than an email to work-at-home moms.

Again, both may be on your lists of prospects or customers, but the marketing messages will be different. Depending on the features of your Customer Relationship Management (CRM) platform or email platform, you can segment your list to make sure each prospect is getting the right information from you.

You probably won't be able to do this type of segmentation right away, and you may even want to move to a more advanced system if you don't have the capability. For example, you'll need a way of assigning customers and prospects to the correct segments. This could mean trying to gather data from them directly that automatically puts them in relevant segments. Or, it could mean assigning them to different segments based on what they download, click, or buy.

Be sure to look at all the capabilities of your current email or CRM platform to see what you can do. And, if you're going to be signing up for a new system, make sure you have the ability to segment your prospects and customers.

3. Language

When creating your profiles and related marketing content, keep in mind that your messages may use different language. For example, single dads may be more responsive to masculine language and sports metaphors than work-at-home moms, as a generalization. Or, social media abbreviations might be much more relevant for teenagers and young adults, while the over 65 crowd may not understand them.

Even something as simple as the pronouns you use in your content can make an impact. For example, if one of your target markets is predominantly female, you'll want to refer to 'she' when talking about something like the use of your product. It will make it instantly relevant to your target customer and make her feel she's included.

When writing marketing content, keep your profiles in mind and make each message different based on the profile you are speaking to. Look back through your data again if you're not sure of the language you should be using. Even more importantly, make a standard list of do's and don'ts when it comes to language used in marketing materials. Make sure anyone creating content for you has a copy of those standards, along with the profiles of your target market.

4. Marketing Channels

The channels you use for delivering your content, communicating your messages, and promoting your offers will also differ depending on the customer profile you're marketing to.

For example, Pinterest has been described as a great social media site for women, but men aren't as present there as they are on other social media sites. Obviously, this isn't a hard and fast rule. Channels like social media change over time, especially as their current audience gets older and their own preferences change.

Use your psychographic profiles when you're doing any major planning as well as when you're choosing channels and tactics. Look for where each of your target customer personas are hanging out online and offline. Look at where they are doing their socializing, research, shopping and buying. Then target your messages to both where they are AND what they're doing in those places.

For example, if your target profile is just looking for ideas on Pinterest, create an ideas board that has links to your content. If they then go to Google to search for an item, make sure you have SEO Optimized content that reflects what they're looking for and the language they use to search for it.

If another segment of your market spends more time on getting social recommendations on Facebook, you might want to focus some of your marketing on getting in front of that group with a giveaway offer or contest. Something that's specifically targeted at solving their problem will definitely get their attention.

5. Sales Copy

You don't have to send everyone to the same sales page. Your promotional content as well as your sales pages and promotional material can be created for each of your unique customer profiles.

Try setting up different landing pages for different segments of your market. Depending on who you're marketing to at the time, use the relevant url for that market. That may mean different ads with different sales copy going to different URL's. It could even mean completely different promotions or list-building giveaways.

Then split test your sales copy in each segment. These A/B tests will tell you what works best for each customer profile. For example, you could set up two versions of the landing page for your single dad profile, and just change the headline in each. When you publish new content or do a promotion that sends people to that landing page, you can use a tool like Google Analytics to analyze one version vs. another.

When you hyper-target your landing page copy this way, you'll likely see a big jump in conversions.

Just remember to always use your customer profiles when writing or creating any type of content for sales pages, emails, products, contests, promotional items and contest prizes. For example, a single dad might be more interested in winning a ticket to a big sports event, while a work-at-home mom may prefer a spa package. That doesn't mean that women don't like sports events, but your profile should tell you this type of information.

As you can see, psychographics take your marketing strategy and tactics to a whole new level. Without this information it's like trying to have the same conversation with your grandma as your teenager. Each person has different goals, experiences, and language that they understand. Psychographic data gives you the power to speak to your listener in a way that they'll respond to.

Strategic Alliances

Word of mouth is one of the most effective ways to grow your business. It's free, or at most costs very little, yet very few businesses use it anywhere near it's potential!

Consider this: if you got just one referral from each one of your customers/clients, over the next 60 days you'd double your client base! What would that mean to your potential income and how many more people would you be helping in supportive and uplifting ways?

So, how do you maximize word of mouth?

Here are 5 Steps you can take now:

1. Really appreciate your customers/clients and let them know consistently you value them

This is the most important, yet overlooked element of creating endless referrals. Many businesses focus more on profits than on people. Focusing on profits alone can be detrimental to success and 'Word of Mouth' success comes from looking beyond just profit into how you can enrich your customer's lives.

Action: At least once a month, take the time to communicate to each of your clients and show them you appreciate them. Send them something of value, something unexpected, a bonus report, a special piece of news you just found. Make it relevant to them and do it regularly. If you keep a CRM database and make a commitment to update it every time you speak to them, you can access it to know what they are interested in! Sprout Social is a great tool that allows you to integrate their social profiles "auto-magically" into the records and track every interaction you have with each contact.

2. Create an exceptional experience each time they deal with you or your company

If you can make doing business with you an exceptional experience, your clients will want to tell a lot of people. People want amazing experiences!

Here is an example: There is an Accountant who has a special relationship with a city coffee shop. Once every 8 weeks he invites his clients to a meeting to chat about industry events related to accounting and their business or finances in general and the coffee and cake is on the house.

Every client that attends gets a card and a voucher from the coffee shop owner to say 'Thank you for joining us today, we would love to see you again soon'. The voucher is a 'buy one get one free' coffee voucher. So they are encouraged to come back again. And because the coffee shop owner is exposing his business to potential new clients the coach pays just cost price on the coffee and cake his clients eat. Normally about 8 clients attend and the cost is around $30. Just a little extra touch can make dealing with your business that much more of an exceptional experience!

Action: What can you do now to add little things that make an exceptional experience? Perhaps you can use the above example or something similar. Remember, start creating exceptional experiences today.

3. Give your customers incentives for giving you referrals

If you're being passive about referrals then you're sitting on a gold-mine. Come up with ways of rewarding your clients for referring business to you. They could receive free gifts, such as a 30 minute back massage voucher for referring a friend or a free hair cut from an award winning beauty salon. The businesses involved would welcome the opportunity to have new clients come their way and would be happy to give that first style cut or treatment for free if they understand the potential value of a new customer.

Bonus: if these businesses are your clients, you win twice!

Action: Reward your clients for referring people to you. Come up with rewards that will be beneficial to your clients. If you worked with executive clients perhaps a free 30 minute health check at a trusted health center would be valuable or a voucher to use at a high-end clothing boutique.

4. Make it easy for clients to give you referrals

If you want to get lots of referrals, you must make it incredibly easy for your clients to tell their friends. Don't expect them to go way out of the way to help you grow your business. Make it as simple as possible.

Action: Develop a "referral package" that you give to your clients. Ask your clients to be an ambassador for your business as you wish to work with people similar to them. The package would include a letter explaining why referrals are important to you, and a series of referral cards that your client can give out to others. Present it professionally and it will hold more value, more worth.

5. Ask at the right time!

When is the best time to ask for referrals? Any time! If you have followed the steps listed above…you've let clients know they are appreciated, you've made dealing with you an exceptional experience, you give them an incentive to share your message with friends and you make it easy for them to do so…you can ask for referrals at any time. Bu this is an important point: The very best time is during your time working with them. Consider a basement remodeling firm; it could take 4-6 weeks to complete the job, correct? During this time, what is one of the most important things on the forefront of the mind of the homeowner? When they are at church, Rotary, daycare or the coffee shop, they are talking about their project. The contractor should be doing such a good job that they feel compelled to introduce them!

CA-TA-SA© System

And when they make it easy to refer them, like the "referral package", the referrals during this 4-6 week timeframe will be very strong.

Action: The key is to do something now. Draft up a letter or e-mail today and just send it off to your clients letting them know how much you value them, who much you have enjoyed working with them in the past and include something that is going to be helpful, useful for them to use, read or understand. Then over the next 4 to 6 weeks develop your 'referral package' and start to use it. Take yourself out of your comfort zone and take action….because if you don't someone will and what will that mean to your business in the years to come.

So now that you have this settled in your business, let's take it to the next level!

Who already has a "Know-Like-Trust" relationship with your Target Audience? If you are trying to do business with electrical engineers for example, it may take a lot of work to get them on the phone to schedule a meeting. But if their Attorney contacted them to invite them to a client-appreciation lunch, they would attend! So, to align yourself with the Attorneys specializing in your specific niche provides a strong connection called "endorsed marketing". You are actually borrowing their credibility! Would you feel confident paying for 10 lunches if they were all your perfect Target Audience? You bet! What's in it for the Attorney? Well, once you meet with them to explain your Competitive Advantage and why you are the obvious choice, they feel comfortable with referring you on a trial basis. You then offer to host a Client Appreciation lunch for their clients in groups of 10. Help them with the invitation, which, of course, highlights the short educational part of the lunch presented by your firm. The topic of the training must include an attention-grabbing headline that they will be interested in. Your presentation should be no longer than 10 minutes with 1-2 actionable steps they can take to accomplish something in their business. Then end it with a call to action of a complimentary phone consultation to see if your services could benefit them further.

Action: Call enough Strategic Alliances that you can set 1 appointment to pitch this idea. Consider the 1st event "practice" and you will learn from it (this takes the pressure off!). Then schedule 1 each and every month. Your business will take off!

Strategic Alliance Marketing Partner Ideas

Company Type

- ❖ Website Owners
- ❖ Trade Associations
- ❖ Professional Schools
- ❖ Retailers
- ❖ Service Providers
- ❖ Corporations

CA-TA-SA© System

- ❖ Local Civic Organizations
- ❖ Manufacturers
- ❖ Magazines
- ❖ Local Print Media

Strategic Marketing Partner Research

1. How long have they been in business?

2. Have they ever done a strategic marketing partnership before?

3. If so, with what companies?

4. Is there any way to get in contact with those companies and speak to them about the success, failure and lessons learned of doing a strategic marketing partnership with your prospective partner?

5. Did they share costs when working with any of these other companies?

6. Would any of the company's you're contacting be open to doing a strategic marketing partnership with you?

7. Do they have a reputation for being honest, professional and doing business the right way?

8. Do they have extensive and successful marketing campaigns?

9. How many contacts do they have in their customer database?

10. Who would you be working with on this project? Decision maker, low-level staff person etc.

11. How can you test the effectiveness and reliability of the partnership before embarking on it full force?

12. What checks and balances would be in place to make sure things are going right?

13. How can either party end the strategic marketing partnership if necessary?

14. Other than a list of prospects or past customers to market to, what does each party bring to the table?

15. How has your strategic marketing partner dealt with conflict in past personal and business relationships?

16. What tracking systems would you put in place to track your success or failure?

CA-TA-SA© System

R4 Framework

    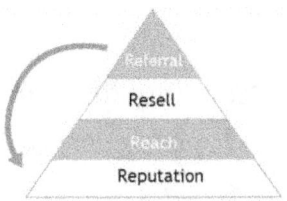

In the Last 10 Years, There Have Been Dramatic Changes in the Marketplace

The competitive landscape for CPA's & Accountants has changed dramatically over the last several years, and will continue to change at an unprecedented pace.

Why? The continued development and distribution of technology has radically changed the way consumers are buying—how they hear about products and services; how they research them; and how they make a final purchase decision.

There are three main drivers of this change that are impacting your business.

You need to be aware of them.

You need to leverage them.

Now let's run through each major driver.

1. Search

*According to Google, 97 percent of consumers search for **local** businesses online. The top 10 organic (non-paid) search results get 95 percent of the clicks.*

First, a look at the numbers. According to recent poll data from the Pew Internet and American Life Project, 92 percent of adult Internet users in the U.S. use a search engine (e.g. Google, Bing) to find information online—with the majority of this group performing keyword searches on a regular basis.

When you look at educated and affluent individuals, search engine use climbs to as high as 98 percent.

These statistics simply underline what you and I already know:

Search is King.

Everyone who has access to the Internet uses a search engine to find relevant and useful information, and according to Google's own data, 97 percent of consumers search for **local** businesses online.

Got visibility?

The upshot of these facts is clear: If you want visibility for your business, you need visibility in the search engines, particularly Google.

Search isn't just king—it's a kingmaker too. High visibility in Google can mean more website traffic, more customers and referrals, more sales activity, and more profit for your business.

And for those business owners in hyper-competitive markets, search-engine visibility can be the difference between being an unknown also-ran and being the Top Dog.

The good, the bad and the ugly: there for all to see

But visibility is a double-edged sword. Customer reviews of your business are visible too.

What if some of these reviews are negative?

What if they're *scathing*?

Well, the bad news is they can haunt your business for years and have a crushing impact on your bottom line.

On the flip side, good reviews can fuel positive word of mouth and generate referral traffic like you've never seen!

Ranking matters

Here's what we know about how people use search engines: after entering a keyword into Google and being presented with pages and pages of blue text links, consumers generally don't dive very deeply into the results (95.91 percent of all clicks occur on page one).

And of page one results, people tend to focus on the top three. According to an Optify study, the top three positions for any given term account for nearly 60 percent (58.5) of the traffic. The top result alone commands an average click-through rate (CTR) of 36.4 percent.

So it's not enough to be "on Google." If you want to take advantage of the popularity of search, your website needs to be listed at the top of the page and above the "scroll line" for the search terms relevant to your business.

2. Social

Businesses have (finally) embraced social media. According to HubSpot, 90 percent of small businesses on Facebook, and 66 percent of them are spending more time on social media than they did a year ago.

We've all heard enough hype about social media to last a lifetime (or two). But there's a good reason, because there's actually something to the hype.

The social web has truly been a game changer.

Suddenly the norm

And the rapid rise of social media is pretty breathtaking.

Just think: Facebook grew from a curiosity in a Harvard dormitory to a global force with over 1,000,000,000 users … in less than a decade.

Facebook seems like old news now—a presence in our lives that we take for granted—but it's worth remembering how recently this shift has taken place.

Study: 59 percent of U.S. consumers use social media to vent about customer care frustrations.

Not just for kids

A common misunderstanding that CPA's & Accountants have is that Facebook and other networks are just for kids, and thus their target market isn't represented demographically on the site.

But the stats tell another story—the opposite story, in fact.

In the U.S., almost two-thirds of all Facebook users are over the age of 35. Recent Pew research reveals that **two-thirds** of U.S. adults use social networking sites like Facebook and Twitter.

High engagement

People aren't just ON social networks. They're GLUED to them.

The average U.S. Facebook user spends a whopping **7 hours and 46 minutes on the site each month**.

That's a full 15.5 minutes the average American spends on Facebook every single day!

The upshot of all of these numbers is pretty straightforward, but I'll spell it out just in case:

Your customers are on Facebook.

They spend a LOT of time there. They're sharing, tweeting, liking, pinning, friending, starring, following, fanning, posting, hash tagging, uploading, retweeting … you name it.

So if you want to reach them, capture their attention and make a pitch for your services before your competitors do … you've got to at least meet them halfway.

Sharing experiences … and frustrations

People are taking to the web to share their experiences with brands, and what they're sharing with their friends and family members isn't always flattering …

According to a study from the Society for Communications Research, 59 percent of U.S. consumers are using social media to **vent** about customer care frustrations. This isn't just happening on Facebook, but on sites like Angie's List, Yelp, Google+ Local and others. According to research from Deloitte, **7 in 10** who read reviews **share** them with friends, family and colleagues, amplifying the impact of these comments even further.

More and more businesses are beginning to realize that, while they can't control what people say online, they can (and should) monitor and contribute to the conversation in an effort to influence the overall tenor.

They're realizing that having a **proactive online presence** that's focused on **adding value to the customer experience** is the surest way to grow and preserve their brand reputation—and protect themselves from the stray musings of a few unhappy souls.

Keeping pace with buyer expectations

Another big reason to get involved in social media is that you have to do it to **stay relevant**.

Your buyers expect it, and if you fall short of their expectations, they'll be more likely to spend their money with the guy down the street.

Even way back in 2008, a Cone Business study on social media found that **93 percent of customers expected companies to have a presence on social channels**, and **85 percent expected companies to interact with them on those social channels**.

That figure has only grown as the social media era has matured.

You can either join the conversation or let your competitors do all the talking.

It's up to you!

3. Mobile ("The really, really big one")

According to research from Mobile Marketer, 70 percent of all mobile searches result in action within one hour!

Look around you: You'll see a steady stream of consumers surfing the web on smartphones, iPads, Nooks, and Kindles.

And this is a trend that's hardly slowing.

It's almost impossible to overestimate the impact of the mobile computing revolution.

In fact, the proliferation of cellphones, smartphones, e-readers and tablet PCs might be one of the most **underestimated** and **under-hyped** shifts in business today.

Today, 87 percent of Americans have mobile phones. It's their No. 1 most-used technology device, with 73 percent saying so versus only 58 percent saying it's their desktop PC.

In their recent Mobile Internet Report, Morgan Stanley projects that mobile browsing will outpace desktop-based access within 3–5 years.

When you pause to consider what these newfangled devices are capable of, and how quickly they emerged from high-priced novelties to ever-present, "can't live without them"[1] gadgets ... it's pretty unbelievable.

SurePayroll.com recently reported: "Accountants Use SMS (Text Message) Marketing During Busy Season. SMS marketing can be used as a communication channel where you send group text messages as reminders about tax filing deadlines, notifications, and time-sensitive items such as payroll. SMS marketing becomes another touch point with clients where your messages can be efficiently produced and delivered and it may prompt them to contact you or take action."

Marc Andreessen, co-creator of Netscape, the first widely used web browser, adds some helpful perspective: "We have never lived in a time with the opportunity to put a computer in the pocket of 5 billion people. Practically everyone is going to have a general purpose computer in their pocket, it's so easy to underestimate that, that has got to be ***the really, really big one.***"

A recent article in the Economist adds this:

> The potential of the smartphone age is deceptive. We look around and see more people talking on phones in more places and playing Draw Something when they're bored. This is just the beginning. In time, business models, infrastructure,

---

[1] To illustrate this point, consider this statistic from Unisys: It takes 26 hours for the average person to report a lost wallet. It takes only 68 minutes for them to report a lost phone.

legal environments, and social norms will evolve, and the world will become a very different and dramatically more productive place.

The revolution will be mobilized

It's clear that the future of the web is tied to smartphones and tablets and other mobile devices. More and more, people who visit your website will do so from a small-screened device instead of a hulking desktop or laptop.

What does that mean to you, the local business owner?

An Asymco study found that people have adopted mobile phone technology faster than almost any other household technology.

It means that if you want an effective web presence that supports your business goals, you need to have a website that supports a multitude of platforms, specifically the smartphone.

In fact, a study from Google found that 6 in 10 mobile users will leave a website if it's not optimized for small screens.

If your business's site looks cramped or cluttered when viewed on a tablet or smartphone, you run the very real risk of turning away your most valuable asset: your customers.

Additionally, <u>43% of emails are read on a mobile device</u>, so if your emails are not formatted for mobile, you are not properly communicating with your clients a and prospects

In a weak economy, mobile matters

Think this "mobile" stuff is much ado about nothing? Let's put this into perspective ...

The economic recovery is a sluggish one. People are still worrying about losing their jobs. Millions of homeowners owe more on their mortgage loans than what their homes are worth. Credit-card debt continues to weigh down U.S. households.

These are challenging times for consumers. As a business owner, you don't want to give them any more reasons not to buy your products or services. Further, you don't want to add any additional friction to the process of buying your products and services!

A streamlined website for mobile is a new must-have. Particularly, when you consider that people with smartphones are still turning to search engines to look for information.

Search to purchase

What's more, studies show that when people use their smartphones to search for information, they're more apt to take immediate action. They search from where they are and go immediately to what they find.

According to research from Mobile Marketer, 70 percent of all mobile searches result in action *within one hour!*

How does your website look and perform on a small screen? What kind of experience are you providing to would-be buyers?

[ ] Good user experience

[ ] So-so user experience

[ ] Poor user experience

What all of this means to YOU!

Alright, readers, let's have a show of hands:

- How many of you search online before deciding what businesses to buy from?

- How many of you choose a company based on the recommendations you heard from friends over social media?

- How many of you carry a smartphone with you at all times?

We all do!

And again, these trends are only accelerating.

As much as we might wish they'd go away and let us continue with business as usual …the search/social/mobile paradigm is not going anywhere. It's here to stay.

The important thing now is to ask the hard questions and seek out the answers—even if they shake things up a bit:

- How do these changes impact the way consumers interact with my business?

- How do these changes impact my business's growth?

- How do these changes impact the way I approach the marketing of my business?

Dramatic Change Calls For ... a Renewed Focus on the Fundamentals!

Given all of these revolutionary changes we've discussed—search, social and mobile—you might be worried that you are going to have to make drastic, revolutionary changes in your business.

That's not necessarily the case.

Our experience shows that *there are four key marketing systems that need to be optimized in order to maximize growth* in today's wired, always-on and hyper-competitive marketplace.

The marketing systems we're about to present aren't even new!

They're proven concepts that have been tested, re-tested and tested again in the marketplace.

Now, sure, some of the tactics have changed, but the strategies themselves haven't.

As it happens, these four essential areas all start with the letter "R."

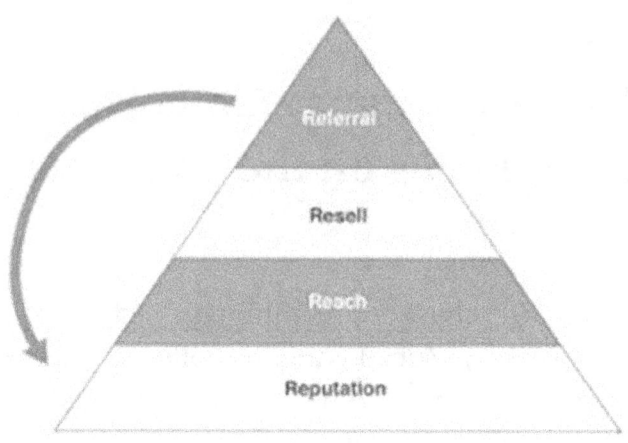

- **Reputation**
- **Reach**
- **Resell**
- **Referral**

These are the four things *every* business needs to plan for and optimize to maximize their growth potential.

Data shows, and my experience proves, that each of these can account for about 25 percent growth on their own, and combined have a compounding effect that can ignite growth to 100 percent or more over a 3-5 year time-frame.

Let's briefly run through each element and explore how maximizing these 4 R's could significantly impact growth at your business.

CA-TA-SA© System

R1: Reputation

What are you doing to proactively manage, protect and monetize your most valuable asset—your reputation?

The first R is **reputation**. As we discussed earlier, it has never been easier for potential customers to find out what others think about your business. This is both good and bad (depending on what people find).

As you know, nowadays people search online before they buy. We know that people put a lot of stock in what they find and read online. In fact, a recent Nielsen study shows that 74 percent of U.S. consumers choose to do business based on online feedback—even when it's feedback from total strangers!

According to Nielsen's summary of their poll data, recommendations from personal acquaintances and opinions posted by consumers online are "the most trusted forms of advertising."

Look who's talking (about you)

A sample of who's talking about your business:

- Customers
- Prospects
- Competitors
- Disgruntled employees
- Ex-spouses
- Former business partners, investors

This probably isn't anything new to you, and there's a decent chance that, like most of the businesses I talk to, you are not very pleased about some of the things people have written about your business!

This brings up a larger point:

Whether it is positive or negative in tone, most of the content about your business that is available online is not even being created by you anymore!

Consumers are critics and publishers now. They all carry tiny "printing presses" in their pockets!

Reputation: more important than ever

To be sure, businesses have always relied on their reputation.

But the stakes are even higher today because of how easy it is for consumers to find information about local companies before they buy.

What's more, as we've already discussed, negative reviews can get lodged in the search results, hanging like an albatross around your neck and dragging down sales.

Are you "Googleable"? How many pages of Google are you on? (You may include Search, Maps, and Google+ Local citations in your answer)

CA-TA-SA© System

[ ] Don't know

[ ] 0

[ ] 1

[ ] 2–5

[ ] 6+

Study:
90 percent of consumers online trust recommendations from people they know; seventy percent trust opinions of <u>unknown</u> users. ~BrightLocal

R2: Reach

What are you doing to ensure that more people know about you today than yesterday?

The second R is reach. It's my experience that a business that wants to grow needs to make sure that more people know about it today than did yesterday.

If you're not meeting new people and telling them about your products and services, you're not developing a pipeline of potential new customers and you are going to see fewer sales in the future as a result.

This sounds pretty obvious, I know. But I'm always surprised when I talk to local business owners and ask them about their promotional efforts.

When I look at the pipeline-filling activities of local businesses, I see mostly a scattershot approach.

A campaign here and there ... with only a vague idea on whether they are getting a positive return on their investment.

No wonder so many businesses become skeptical of marketing:

They're doing it wrong!

Very rarely do I see coordinated, systematic and metrics-driven efforts to reach a wider audience and drive more prospects (i.e. people who are interested in what you're selling) through the front door.

But this kind of focused, ongoing and intentional approach is exactly what's necessary to reach more qualified prospects in a cost-effective—not to mention satisfying!—manner.

A once-in-awhile, ad hoc marketing strategy is not going to get the results you need to achieve consistent business growth.

Do you have a method to build a continually growing prospect/client email list?

CA-TA-SA© System

[ ] Yes

[ ] No

[ ] We don't have a list

R3: Resell

What are you doing to upsell, cross sell and repeat sell to maximize the lifetime value of your customer base?

The third R is **resell**. Once you've done all of the hard and often costly work of getting a customer, you need to make sure to maximize the lifetime value, or LTV, of that customer.

Whatever metaphor you want to use ... mining your backyard ... picking the low hanging fruit ... the point is the same:

It makes more sense (both financially and from an efficiency standpoint) to fully capitalize on your existing customer base than to be constantly on the hunt for new customers.

The more value you can generate from each customer, the less you have to spend on marketing, which means you can increase your profit margins and/or reinvest the savings into your products and services—in the process making your business even more attractive to your customers!

In practice, this can mean increasing the dollar value of each transaction or increasing the frequency that customers buy, either by offering add-on services or upsells or cross-sells.

McDonald's offers the classic example: 'Do you want fries with that?' 'Do you want to supersize your order?'

These days there are so many cost effective and trackable ways to bring customers back to your business.

To give you just one example, consider an email and/or SMS coupon campaigns. Average redemption rates of 20 percent or more, it potentially costs less than 30 cents per customer in your door!

Despite having easy access to new and cool tools, most business in our area are leaving money on the table because they're not maximizing the resell potential of each customer.

Do you ethically (but effectively) prepare buyers from their very first purchasing experience with you to keep coming back to purchase over and over again?

[ ] No

[ ] Yes

R4: Referral

What are you doing to use your successful relationships to create new, organic opportunities so that you can spend less and make more?

The fourth R is **referral**.

Since you're doing such a great job taking care of your customers and keeping them happy, the next best thing you can do is set up systems to maximize the benefit you get from them, right? So that they are doing the marketing for you!

Well, it's well known that if you just leave it up to people to do referrals for you, very few will—even if they are very happy with you.

You have to make it very easy—almost effortless—for your happy customers to refer your business if you really want to maximize the referrals you generate from them.

A study from Lee Resource Inc. found that attracting a new customer can cost five times as much as keeping an existing one.

Referrals make great customers

We all want referrals because they help us save money on marketing, right?

Well, there's even more to gain from referrals than cost savings:

According to a case study noted in the Harvard Business Review, customers that come from referrals are, on average, about 18 percent more likely than others to stay with a company and they generate 16 percent more in profits!

And according to several case studies reported on by the website TechCrunch:

Friends referred by friends make better customers.

They spend more (a 2x higher estimated lifetime value than customers from all other channels at One Kings Lane); **convert better** (75 percent higher conversion than renters from other marketing channels at Rent the Runway); and **shop faster** (they make their first purchase after joining twice as quickly than referrals from other channels at Trendyol).

Why are referrals so powerful?

Because they channel the power of **social proof**. Social proof is a fancy way of saying that we humans are easily influenced by each other.

CA-TA-SA© System

When a member of our pack (family) or tribe (social circle) recommends a product or service, we take that recommendation very seriously.

Similarly, when someone in a position of power, prestige or authority recommends something, we are very **quick to act** on that recommendation.

You see the applied power of social proof everywhere: in TV ads, when you see a celebrity endorsing a product; on the radio, when the person hosting the pledge drive tells listeners that so-and-so donated $50 to NPR; on the back of a novel you're reading, when you see testimonials from other notable authors; and on the web, when you visit sites like Yelp.com to read consumer reviews of local restaurants.

Moving from passive to active, ad hoc to systematic

Almost without fail, most businesses I talk to have no clear referral generation system.

They essentially think that referrals are something that you simply wait and hope for ... but the reality is that referrals don't just happen; you have to go out and get them!

And if you're going to spend the time collecting them, you need a system that effectively channels your efforts into tangible results.

How many formal, written referral-generating systems do you currently have with prospects or potential partners? (Check one)

[ ] 0

[ ] 1

[ ] 2–5

[ ] 6+

What are you missing?

Now, the problem is that most businesses are operating without even being aware of these changes or marketing systems, and how it is impacting their business.

Let me give you some examples ...

First, if you aren't effectively and proactively managing your reputation, you aren't aware of negative comments being made about your business:

Negative review? Ouch. That hurts. Comments will negatively impact how others view your business in the marketplace. According to Nielsen, user reviews are "the most trusted form of advertising."

Or, you have people looking for your business on their mobile phones, and your website is showing up where the visitor must scroll over and up and down just to view your site!

No one has fingers small enough (or patience long enough) to navigate this web page. A study from Google found that 60 percent of users will leave a website if it's not optimized for mobile.

People will stay on your competitor's website if it's optimized for a small touchscreen.

So, how can we address some of these things?

Let me share some ideas … I obviously can't give you all of them in the space of this small book, but let me share a few:

- Control your own reviews with your own review site

- Create a separate mobile site for your business that is optimized for mobile

- Reach more people more cost-effectively and with greater targeting using Facebook ads

Is your business being left behind?

Now, if you fall into the category of businesses that are not proactively working with these technology changes and marketing systems, **you are only going to see things get worse over time**.

These changes, though recent, are now a permanent part of the competitive landscape.

The gap between the businesses that "get it" and those that don't is widening at an accelerating pace.

You can look at any industry and see examples of the handful of businesses that are really pulling away from the pack, and those that are falling behind.

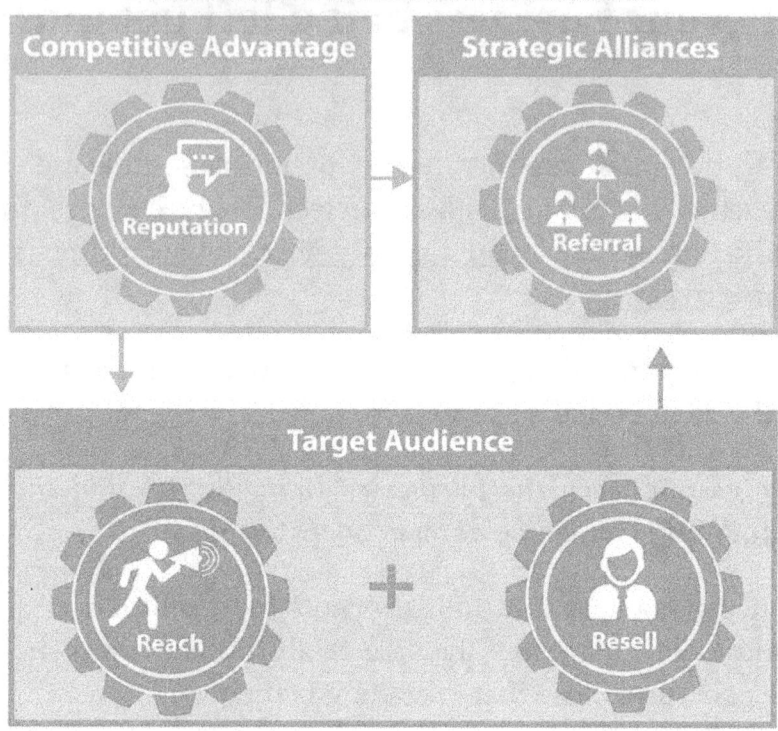

It's time to go 'all-in'

Do you have someone that is helping your business in these areas?

Or are you kidding yourself into thinking that you are going to try to do this by yourself or with the very part-time effort of one of your employees that has no marketing background?

That's not going to cut it.

If you're struggling to fit everything into your calendar already (most business owners I talk to are), you're probably not going have the bandwidth to optimize the four R's. Either something else has to give, or you need to enlist a friendly expert to help you!

Answer the call

Get this: according to data from Google, **61 percent of local searches on a mobile phone result in a phone call**.

Are you ready, both literally and figuratively, to answer that call?

Or are you going to let ring until one of your competitors picks up the phone?

Are you ready to answer the call? Or are you going to let ring until one of your competitors picks up the phone?

What Are You Doing to Optimize the Four R's?

Reputation: *What are you doing to proactively manage, protect and monetize your most valuable asset—your reputation?*

_____

_____

_____

Reach: *What are you doing to ensure that more people know about you today than yesterday?*

_____

_____

_____

Resell: *What are you doing to upsell, cross sell and repeat sell to maximize the lifetime value of your customer base?*

_____

_____

_____

Referral: *What are you doing to use your successful relationships to create new, organic opportunities so that you can spend less and make more?*

_____

_____

_____

If you're ready to make a shift ...

You may realize that you need to make a change, that you aren't growing like you should, that your current approach to marketing is not working, and that you are committed to getting past your current income limits.

If so, I would be interested in talking with you to see if there is potentially a good fit to work together.

However, I must say upfront that I only work with one CPA or Accountant per zip code so I can give them all of my knowledge and experience without having to worry about conflict with another client.

And I am particular about who I work with.

I work with firms that are already successful and are looking for strategic ways to get FAR MORE successful.

I work with clients that have the mindset and resources to handle the level of growth that is possible to achieve.

What to do next

If you've seen the benefit of what you've read in these pages, then I'd encourage you to contact us immediately. From there, we will set up a follow up phone call interview to see if we are a good fit to work together.

This phone conversation is not a guarantee that we will work together. But it is a necessary first step if we are to work toward achieving the growth you're capable of.

How to connect: Select a time that fits your schedule for a 15 minute phone call: www.MarketingHuddle.com/contact-mike

From there, if you and I both agree that there may be a good potential fit, I will offer you a 360 degree Marketing Audit on your practice. This will identify your current strengths and weaknesses to optimize your business growth. The Audit is a $250 consultation and I am offering a limited amount at no cost.

I look forward to hearing from you!

Mike Saunders, MBA
Business Strategist | Marketing Fanatic
Mike@MarketingHuddle.com
www.MarketingHuddle.com
www.Linkedin.com/in/MikeSaundersMBA

www.ingramcontent.com/pod-product-compliance
Lightning Source LLC
Chambersburg PA
CBHW051736170526
45167CB00002B/959